Community Places
Hospital

by Amy McDonald

CHOC Children's Hospital

THE BILL HOLMES TOWER

BLASTOFF! Beginners

BELLWETHER MEDIA
MINNEAPOLIS, MN

Blastoff! Beginners are developed by literacy experts and educators to meet the needs of early readers. These engaging informational texts support young children as they begin reading about their world. Through simple language and high frequency words paired with crisp, colorful photos, Blastoff! Beginners launch young readers into the universe of independent reading.

Blastoff! Universe

Reading Level — Grade K

Grades 1-3

BLASTOFF! DISCOVERY — Grade 4

Sight Words in This Book 🔍

a	get	new	this
an	go	on	to
and	had	people	we
are	help	see	well
at	here	the	
come	is	there	

This edition first published in 2022 by Bellwether Media, Inc.

No part of this publication may be reproduced in whole or in part without written permission of the publisher. For information regarding permission, write to Bellwether Media, Inc., Attention: Permissions Department, 6012 Blue Circle Drive, Minnetonka, MN 55343.

Library of Congress Cataloging-in-Publication Data

Names: McDonald, Amy, author.
Title: Hospital / by Amy McDonald.
Description: Minneapolis, MN : Bellwether Media, 2022. | Series: Community places | Includes bibliographical references and index. | Audience: Ages PreK-2 | Audience: Grades K-1
Identifiers: LCCN 2021044369 (print) | LCCN 2021044370 (ebook) | ISBN 9781644875667 (library binding) | ISBN 9781648346576 (paperback) | ISBN 9781648345777 (ebook)
Subjects: LCSH: Hospitals--Juvenile literature. | Hospital care--Juvenile literature. | Medical personnel--Juvenile literature.
Classification: LCC RA963.5 .M35 2022 (print) | LCC RA963.5 (ebook) | DDC 362.11--dc23
LC record available at https://lccn.loc.gov/2021044369
LC ebook record available at https://lccn.loc.gov/2021044370

Editor: Christina Leaf   Designer: Andrea Schneider

Printed in the United States of America, North Mankato, MN.

Table of Contents

At the Hospital! 4

What Are Hospitals? 6

Help at the Hospital 10

Hospital Facts 22

Glossary 23

To Learn More 24

Index 24

At the Hospital!

Mom had a baby.
We are at
the hospital!

What Are Hospitals?

Hospitals are helpful places. Doctors and nurses work there.

nurse

doctor

People go
to the hospital
to get care.

Help at the Hospital

This is a waiting room. People wait to see a doctor.

waiting room

This is an **exam** room. Nurses check on people.

exam room

This is the **emergency room**. People come here to get help fast.

emergency
room

This is a hospital room. People **recover** here.

hospital room

This is
the **nursery**.
New babies
sleep here.

new
baby

nursery

Hospitals help people get well!

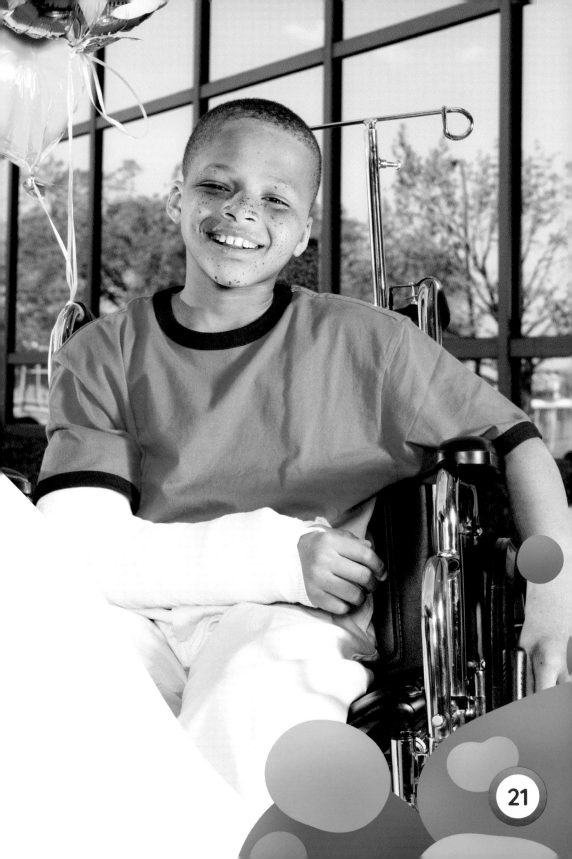

Hospital Facts

Inside a Hospital

doctor nurse

exam room

What Happens in a Hospital?

get an exam recover from being sick have a baby

Glossary

emergency room

part of a hospital where people get help quickly

exam

check up

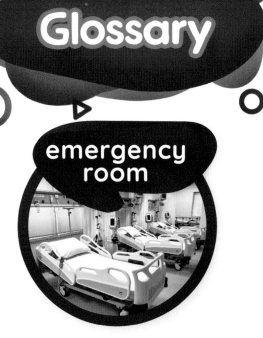

nursery

a room where babies sleep

recover

to get better

To Learn More

ON THE WEB

FACTSURFER

Factsurfer.com gives you a safe, fun way to find more information.

1. Go to www.factsurfer.com.

2. Enter "hospital" into the search box and click 🔍.

3. Select your book cover to see a list of related content.

Index

baby, 4, 18
care, 8
doctors, 6, 7, 10
emergency
  room, 14, 15
exam room, 12
help, 6, 14, 20
hospital room,
  16

mom, 4
nursery, 18, 19
nurses, 6, 12
recover, 16
sleep, 18
waiting room,
  10, 11
work, 6

The images in this book are reproduced through the courtesy of: Ken Wolter, front cover; Ridofranz, p. 3; Monkey Business Images, pp. 4-5, 12-13, 22 (inside); Krakenimages.com, p. 6; Roman Chazov, pp. 6-7; freemixer, pp. 8-9; sturti, pp. 10-11; New Africa, p. 12; cleanfotos, p. 14; SDI Productions, pp. 14-15; Suwin, p. 16; Gorodenkoff, pp. 16-17; Tatyana Vyc, p. 18; MikeDotta, pp. 18-19; wavebreakmedia, p. 20; FangXiaNuo, pp. 20-21; Lordn, p. 22 (exam); ESB Professional, p. 22 (recover); FamVeld, p. 22 (have a baby); f28production, p. 23 (emergency room); didesign021, p. 23 (exam); Randy Duchaine/ Alamy, p. 23 (nursery); Tempuera, p. 23 (recover).